# The Strategist #21

# Quick And Easy Rules of Strategies

## By

## Melvin Lightford Ministries, INC.

authorHOUSE™

*1663 Liberty Drive, Suite 200*
*Bloomington, Indiana 47403*
*(800) 839-8640*
*www.AuthorHouse.com*

*First published by AuthorHouse 08/15/05*

*ISBN: 1-4184-4377-8 (sc)*

*Library of Congress Control Number: 2004094008*

*Printed in the United States of America*
*Bloomington, Indiana*

*This book is printed on acid-free paper.*

1st Step You must do is believe in yourself.

2nd Step How do you think?

3rd Step What level are you?

4th Step Are you a positive person?

5th Step Are you compatible?

6th Step Are you versatile?

7th Step Are you ambitious?

8th Step Are you determined?

9th Step Are you confident?

10th Step Are you prepared?

11th Step What is your potential?

12th Step What are your strengths and
Weaknesses?

13th Step Do you have a desire to learn?

14th Step Do you have the will to learn?

15th Step Are you a caring person?

16th Step Do you know right from wrong?

# Words Of Wisdom

Self-motivating factors and how to succeed in life will place your accomplishments within reach.

The questions that are asked in the book can show you the way for a positive outlook and that how you think, does determine who you are.

May the questions and answers I've given to you from my own  word bring you success. By having known how, ability and the insight are the keys.

What does it take to be a strategist? Believe the problem has an outcome before it can be given the answer. I continue by saying no matter what the problem is, if you have a plan, you can overcome the problem by coming up with ways for planning a strategy to counter anything you come up against. Then you notice anything that is not correct in your assessment. Then you go back in with a new outlook and you look to find what other ways or avenues there are for implementing another criteria.

That can challenge your inner thought process through finding other ways to get positive and substantial results. If not enough, be aware of your circumstances and surroundings and make a better move toward mechanisms that you have used in past procedures to counter anything coming in or going out at you.

# Words From The Author

The book starts by talking about questions and answers that can be of help to you. These questions answers give you the insight to know, and help you to know how success can come your way if you are willing to put in the hard work. To be successful is not easy but can be assured if you give it a try and have the might. Just be happy enough to the challenge in knowing that if you put in the time?

# Table of Contents

# Chapter 1

The first step is believe in yourself.

When you don't believe in yourself, what you are actually saying is you don't believe you can do the things that you think if it is negative; deny it and move on to positive thinking. Only you can decide if you are negative by the way you handle different things that occur in your life. I say, believe you can do anything your heart desires, but know that it is truly up to you: No one else can tell you otherwise. Belief in the word "Believe" will help you with part of your vocabulary. This is the word that is going to get you over, the hump in the road. I say think, think some more, then brain storm with some ideas of your own, that have been on your mind. Do what is necessary to adjust and implement, using the marketing tools that are available, as well as needed, to bring you into a positive thinking mode. Never say never, but think positive by being constructive to the facts even those you are not doing anything in particular. This keeps you on the right track for progress to be made.

How you think is where you are at in your life, so don't blame others for your misfortune, just go back out and look at your situation with hope and go after what is rightfully yours. They say believing in yourself is half the battle; I believe this to be true to a certain degree.

But the circumstances that you face have a lot to do with self. Be able to adapt and thus find your way clear. Adjusting to "everyday" life and coming up with a daily plan is important for you to be able to change and make changes that are needed for the situation to warrant that change to come about. I can see myself a winner and a doer in accomplishing what I must do in keeping self; again in a constructive frame of mind to do what is proper and  oppose what is not proper. To be the believer, you must see yourself as truly having a vision and a keen eye knowing what your true intention or objective might be or will be, is a matter of pursuing that objective to put it into the past or bring it into a reality. The vision or how you think indeed will have effect on where you are in your life. Think good things, in whatever you undertake in your life, and go for them by believing they were the things you had to do to bring them all together. The capabilities that are in you are because something in your life triggers what you were supposed to be doing at that given time, or a situation interferes, then it  purpose to your life and it is up to you until a certain point. There's no getting around the purpose if you know where you are going in your life. Think out loud  on where you just may want to be, then go and do it. Stop resisting and again believe in that what you are doing is for the better. Look for progress in your life and seek and find those solutions you need to corroborate and make sure you were doing what you needed to do to enable you to accomplish the necessities of life. See yourself as a leader and go, pursue that goal by reaching for the sky; don't let anyone stop you from getting your share, called success.

Take some risk; they are known to be good or bad, but it is part of the learning jargon. Nothing comes easy in life unless you were born with a golden spoon in your mouth. How you perceive things that are happening in your life, like it or not, they do affect who you are and what others see you as. I say, don't worry about what other people think of you, stay focused and do what is necessary for you to survive by having a game plan. You did believe in the plan and with God's help it came to pass.

People like making excuses when all else fails, but it's the individual that must make the adjustment for the time being, which guides him or her to doing what is apparently right for that moment.

When there are obstacles in one's life we cannot dwell on those. We live and learn by past mistakes. Move on to climbing higher heights that are within a reasonable distance. Thinking big along the way gives you the needed inspiration for that journey to be a successful one. How many of you think someone is going to give you something for nothing? I say believe you can do the things your heart knows you can do, and set your goals high: Obtain those goals because they were within reach after all. This is part of dreaming, and when you dream, dream that success is coming, that it's just a matter of time called persistence.

In life there's a beginning stage and an ending stage. You better know the difference between the two. Be a believer, remind yourself change is coming and never give into the pressure of your everyday life. Motivate yourself by pulling up your pant straps, continue getting out there, and perform to the best of your ability.

# Chapter 2

The second step, "how you think" will either put you over the top or down on the bottom for instance, don't go around with a negative disposition. This can hurt you beyond anything you can imagine. You want to be seen with a positive image, doing things that are right and you want to be seen as a company person who looks out for the company. How you look at life's circumstances will determine where you are in your life and if you have the drive to achieve what you really want to do with your life. Are you in control of your life or do you have to be taught, told every thing you do? Are you a leader. Can your boss and co-workers trust you? Will they listen to you? Can you get their undivided attention ? Are you a winner or loser? You tell me. It up to each and everyone of us to answer this question for ourselves alone. After all everybody is an individual. When you're on the top of things can you be productive for the company? Can you find ways to staying on the top? Do you have good marketing skills; can your management skills be put to good use?

# Chapter 3

At what level of management are you? Can you go higher from mid-management level? Do you have good communication skills? Can you cope? Whether the company is growing or not at anticipated levels, can you accept the lows and highs of the company? Can you relate to the people around you, co-workers? Keep your mind contained with good thoughts and don't let anything that isn't of righteousness be in you. Stay around influential people-they are the ones who will encourage you because they usually want to see others succeed. When it comes to learning you need to be doing what is right now in life, to bring growth, understanding. Everybody goes through something in their life; Don't let it get you down, just move on to doing something else, that you are capable of doing and be happy living your life, enjoying what you're doing for the better.

Know this for sure-everyone that you come in contact within your lifetime is not your friend. They are out to finding out what you can do for them, and if you  cannot do something for them, they will depart soon from you, go after someone else and they will do the same thing to them. Count your blessings that they departed. It's for the better, they were never a true friend. Having focus is a key to your success and you need to keep a good frame of mind. Believing what you think is the correct way. It does help you to overcome.

# Chapter 4

Are you a positive person? Can you accept the challenges of life that you need to, in adjusting to staying that way? Your life will reflect whether you are a positive thinking person or not, and you need to know, the sooner the better. What make a person stay positive in their life? Not watching a lot of cable television. This keep out all the negatives things; thoughts that are going around in the world. What this does is keep your head from being filled with unnecessary thoughts that are not conducive to learning. Also having goals in life keeps you on the right track, keep you thinking logical and practical and focused on doing things in your life that are beneficial. Your environment is the key: By not being around those people who aren't caring or those people who don't have goals to achieve things that are supposed to be of magnitude. Your life must be a life of producing and seeing achievements, you will see growth by having your life's desire and doing things that makes you happy. How you feel is a determining factor in what you think. Your health is a major issue, which factors in how you think and what you think, so keep his in mind. They say life can be what you want it to be, but on the other and it's different for sure. There's an old saying I believe they say what in the box is not necessarily what is? When you think positive, it enables you to be creative and distinctive in your thinking.

Whether these things can come together is a different story altogether. Negative thoughts come from a bad attitude gathered all together, they define who you are. If you seem to be a complainer, it is without a doubt that you don't really know how to reason because selfish, desirable ways got in the way. Resisting what was right, doing what was wrong satisfied your ways. I say listen and believe in the right way, discontinue the wrong way of doing things. How you select whether something is of your choosing. Don't blame others for your failure and dilemmas of life. Look at life with hope, worthiness, and live your life accordingly with positive approaches, even when all things may not be going well. Think positive thoughts, leave negative things behind you. Learn not to argue or ever let someone put you in a vulnerable situation where you cannot see your way clear. Don't argue, It's a no brainier. To tell you the truth, it's not worth peanuts and two wrongs don't make a right. Be determined in life and never be afraid to fail. Stay in the fight and regain what you have lost.. Get back out there and believe once again in Yourself that you will make it. No one owes you anything. Whether you were born back then or now, go out there and get your share, do what is right. Continue to live life but don't hang with losers. Move on. There is so much to live for when you're doing things to the best of your ability. Everybody does not make the same pay and they never, ever will. The playing field by far isn't fair. It never will be but it no excuse for you. I mention this to you because it does matter if you really want something out of your life. It is by thinking big, not small, that maybe you might just like what you see in yourself that leads you to be persistence.

# Chapter 5

Are you compatible with others? If you know you are compatible with others, then you must be. We can all say we are compatible in our lives with the people around us that we know and see daily, that are part of our lives. This I believe determines where you stand in your life.

Can you work with other people outside of your environment that you think you are compatible with? Only time will tell and that is the difference. I say live and learn and do what it takes in getting along with them. We cannot make people like us. If they do fine. If not don't worry. Many people in the world aren't. This is  known fact. Some people are compatible, otherwise you are not going to have any customers. What are you going to do then? Complain and say you don't have any customers because you can not get along with them? This would be very strange indeed. Whether male or female, you and I have to get along in today's society more than ever because of the different types of jobs and the fact there are men as well women who are in supervisory or management positions. Like it or not, I say welcome to modern times, you are going to have both male and female bosses.

# Chapter 6

Are you versatile? This can be the best
thing that could ever happen to you if you are.
I say this because it makes you more valuable
as an employee, knowing multiples jobs makes
you more money in the long run. People can say
they can do this job or that job, but when it come
down to it, are your skills adequate for what
the job calls for? Yes or no? Think about what
I just said and think about what I really mean.
The reason why we know so much a lot of times
is because when we were younger, we took
chances by experimenting to see if we could
actually do something. We did not want to get
the training but we tried these things because
they were different; a challenge to us as children

growing up. It was part of seeking and finding something to do or what have you. When you're versatile you are somewhat smarter  than the average Joe. Without hesitation I would say this is true. My reasoning is that I believe you had the will to learn at a young age and that for some reason it carried over to your adult life. Now you use those abilities to succeed in life, which makes it much easier to accept those changes that are coming in your lifetime. One way or another a change will take place in your life. It may be when you're in your twenties, thirties, or forties. Change is coming. I say if you adapt to life, you can change, and they say, is a good thing because it brings a new approach, a new outlook on life in general because you've been given a fresh start.

# Chapter 7

Are you ambitious? Yes, and as a matter of fact, what I've done in my life could have only happen by the grace of God. Thankful, I am yes; appreciated, yes; grateful, yes. I can honestly say when the Lord gave out the talents he did not shortchange me in any way, shape or form. To be ambitious doesn't come  overnight. You must work every facet of your life, and be a doer, and put in the time to learn what is right. You must pursue what you think you want to do, not letting anybody else's agenda keep you from accomplishing the personal goals that you have set for yourself. The key to be ambitious is to be established. If You are, this is a jump start for you to be successful in accomplishing

what you deem is necessary for you to get there.
Another factor-stay focused and Associate only
with positive, successful people In general,
this will keep you on the right track to success.
Think this is good for you. Every chance you
get day- dream a little, you'll be glad you did.
When brainstorming , this is how you get the
information needed out of you, because it is
hidden in your brain and you must recall what is
there for the asking.

Remember the key to learning is thinking,
then doing what you need to do, to get you to
that next level which should be your "almost"
goal. Climbing the corporate ladder is what you
should want to do. Getting there takes time and
desire, and the bottom-line you can achieve.

# Chapter 8

Are you determined? One way you can
tell a winner is by what is going on in his life and
how he tackles the situations that come up and
occur simultaneously in his or her life. Also, if
there was or is adversity, can you sustain where
you are going in life; whether you can allows the
ordeals and tribulations of life to rule over you or
not, is the deciding factor. To be determined in
life is proving yourself to, God that you thank him
for your God-given ability or abilities that could
have only come  from Him. This also builds on
confidence for you to accept the challenges of
life and pursue what you need to do. For you to
accomplish, you must desire to be a winner, not
a loser. We all know someone in question who

is a loser but the bottom-line is you don't want to be known as a loser. I challenge you right now to believe in yourself. Do what is required of you knowing that  success is within reach and that you can get there within reasonable expectation by obtaining the know how for success.

It's up to you, not me-you! Where you are in your life now is where you were supposed to be: Now you can change this with success. We can all want this and that but can you go out and do what you need to do in achieving that goal or are you all talk and no action? There are lots of people like that in everyday life, and the bottom-line again, the number one excuse, is the blame game or human error. I have been around many people in my life and I've found many of them with one skill, and I say to myself "wow, if something ever happened they have been one dimensional. They wonder why they cannot cope with life situations. They underestimated their own skill levels for wanting to learn."

# Chapter 9

Are you confident? You better be or you will never taste success. If you look it in  the eye it is going to leave you in a hurry. Your hope is the confidence to want things to get done. Otherwise there's nothing  happening after all. It was for not. Life is what you make of it, so stop making excuses. Time does build confidence but we all have a lifetime to achieve. Not knowing when that time is up should remind us to do the things we need to do and reach for the sky, never allowing limitations to be put  or brought upon us. When you do your job are you confident that you're doing the right thing or are you guessing your confident? If so, why? I strongly believe if you are confident enough you can do anything and all things because you chose to put your mind to the task. In our daily lives and where we live every time the door opens up we walkout with confidence. Because we're doing things that are of culture and are constructive to our well-being, it enables us to be confident.

# Chapter 10

Are you prepared? There is an old scout motto, "Be prepared" This makes sense.

Everyday you live is a challenge. Whether you are or not, don't blame someone else for you not being prepared  in your life. There are the lows and highs. Get used to them: They're coming in bunches. Get with the program people and believe in yourself, do what is right. Look ahead, keep your head high, it can only get better. When something is at a low in your life, don't stay there. Think and get back in the race. It happen to me, and I am sharing this with you. To be organized you must want to be, and if you aren't it does reflect on you and people around you are going to see it. You can  be sure they're going to be talking about you so don't look around. I have never been so prepared in my life. I'm living now, without a doubt at the best time for me. The future looks brighter than I anticipated. After all success is looking me right in the face. When you are organized, even if you don't know something, just by being organized makes you a winner; People always want to be around winners. We can all be a winner if we take the time to do things and put in the hard work to achieve success. When it comes, it is contagious. If you truly want to be somebody you can. You can't worry about what someone is saying  about you. Go ,do what you must do and imply the knowledge. Before you know I success will come. If you need help by all means higher a consultant, they're affordable. Do have the expertise to show you how.

The more experience you have, the better off you are because this helps you develop your skills whether they are in marketing, management, personnel or industrial. They all can consolidated. If you are not prepared, how

can you make a living by not being prepared?
How else are you going to pay. Your bills. So it
only right that you would go to work.

When you are prepared it make you an
optimist, because your thinking is valid. You're
anticipating  something usually happening good,
and it does because you were already there.

# Chapter 11

What is your potent ional ? First of all, it has to do with you, whether you place limitations on yourself depends upon what you think of yourself. Your potent ional is what you think that matters, and I believe it also depends upon your capabilities. They say the more you know is what you're worth, but is this always the truth? I say no! Also the potent ional that you have hasn't been tapped yet, because it depends on your age and the level of education, what you know. When it comes to talents, these other bargaining tools, which can be beneficial to any employer. Another factor-how you think on your feet has a lot to do with what you know. Can you respond to pressure situations? Potentional is anything that can be retained by you, and used to enhance your skills to produce something that is of legitimate significance. We are all at different levels. For our potent ional to kick in. If and after all is said and done, if we get there fine, if not, we didn't really understand. We must tap into our memory bank and resources to allow the things that are there to come out of us? Whether they can take us to another level-line. If not, it was never meant to be after all, or not to have taken place in our lives. Potentional. It can be basically anything you can do that is of a constructive nature that is within reason.

You could say potent ional comes from within and either you have it or you don't. It's something that is obviously in you and to bring it out of you I guess you can call this fortitude. Many people have it but few of them know how to use it.

I believe if you want to know the purpose for your life here on the earth right now, I say prayed and ask God what your true purpose is. Then I believe you will know and understand what it is you're supposed to be doing with your life. This then helps  defines you knowing  where you stand, and whether or not you need to make sacrifices. People are afraid to find out what they really know verses what they don't know, so they will never reach their full potent ional until they realize there are some limitations on knowledge. Don't take this as a negative word or rejection. Not everyone is smart, like it or not, we know this. So why fool yourself? If you know deep down inside you want something, then go for it. If you don't succeed always there's next time. There shall come a time in your life where beginning is the starting gate. Open up the gate and get going. What is on the other side is your hope because you took the initiative to find out. By taking a chance you were able to see beyond a reasonable doubt that you tried, you never let failure enter the picture.

# Chapter 12

What are your strengths and weaknesses? My strengths are that I call on the name of Jesus everyday of my life, and I thank God for allowing me to do the things I do for him. These are my strengths. My strengths come from anything that I am good at that pertains to my credentials, whether management, public relations, product development, merchandising, cost effectiveness, sales, inventories, advertising, purchasing, budgeting. There's much more but I don't have to name them all, you get the picture. Your strength can be anything that been a particular, positive influence in your life. People in general will say they did this and that but really don't tell you anything. My strengths are doing what I need to get done, accomplishing what I have set out to do. This enables me to pursue and go after the things I need  in solving problems and situations that arise. My strength is my mind-being able to achieve that which gives me balance in  my life right now. I can perceive and do what is right in the eye of the beholder, the things that are necessary for me to be successful. When you have strengths you can offset weaknesses because they are hidden. Your strengths are anything and everything that produces something indirect or direct. The strengths you display must be able to get you out of those things that are not right. I continue to say your strengths can be further used as anything that gives you a positive drive which motivates you in succeeding. Weaknesses are anything that isn't producing for you. What they do is cause relapses and than you become stale. Weaknesses are things that are quantity instead of quality. You can be sure they're of times different. Just look at life situations when they say it was like this and not that. Weaknesses are usually seen when you don't have any idea on what you're doing. You tried to hide the weaknesses because you have been exposed, which is usually unintentional. Lots  of times weaknesses are discovered by accident. This is when you'll find out the truth that someone has been hiding from you. Weaknesses put limits on you because they just do. We all have some weaknesses. Let just face the facts and move on to do something different.

# Chapter 13

Do you have a desire to learn?

We all have a desire to learn and whether we do has to do with us as individuals. When you stop learning I think you're giving up on life itself. So stay away from people like that and associate with people that you can learn from. Many family members you can honestly learn from. It's just a matter of time and how much time you, your relatives spend together as family, whether or not you can go to them for some type of help. Learning is just like one, two and three. What you see is what you usually get, so learn what you can. The will make you want to learn; It should come natural because it's part of our survival skills that are embedded in us from birth, through childhood and into adulthood. Without the will to learn we would be in trouble as human beings. I say accept the challenge and learn what you can now early in life and when you get older it will carry over. In life something come easier than others but you don't make up excuses because you didn't know it. So if you tried something that you had little inclination to do but than you realized it was not for you after all. We do have the power to control everything we learn as people or we can object to what we are being taught and we do this by complaining to someone who will listen to us. The bottom-line in learning comes from being self-motivated. If you are this is a good thing because you're focused to what happening around you.

The opposite of motivated- the word I use is laziness. I don't even want to go there because it a negative. Again, having the will to learn comes from a positive attitude and the desire to pursue what in your heart. You must think to become creative. Knowing can make you create anything. This is left up to you. Either you want

something out of life or you don't, and it going
to cost you so why not take the chance now,
do what it takes. If we look back on our lives to
see what we have gone through don't you think
it would tell us something about ourselves? It is
so important to learn because after all, it is how
we see you daily in life. If that is not right, don't
friend or family member might say something on
your behalf. Wake up, smell the coffee and lead
a life that can be fulfilled. I go, on to say reach
for the sky and do the things you love best and
don't worry. Half the battle is seeing ourselves
do the right thing. I go on to say, never give in or
up, be yourself.

# Chapter 14

Do you have the will to learn?

You must have a will to learn that what is right or wrong is up to you. A will to desire that no matter what comes or what it takes, you are going to be there make it all happen. You have to decide now is the time, you're not going to let anyone stand in your way. Hard work takes these few things-anticipating, forecast, research and instinct. If you have these they will carry you through no doubt. The will should be to become established and then only can you see your way clear. It takes time, takes patience, but you can do it. Just getting up in the morning is a will to learn because what you do. You're looking at yourself everyday you go into the bathroom. There is a mirror, this mirror appears to be watching you one way or another. And you know, it's reminding you who you are. Like it or not, the image in the mirror is you  and there's no getting around that. Speaking about your will should wake you up and tell you something. Do I want to stay this way for five, ten, may be fifth teen years depends on you and where you want to go. Think about what I stated and close your eyes for one minute. You'll be surprised what is going to come to your mind. Everything we do in our lives is predicated on how we think and whether those intentions are good or bad does decide your present and future. Your will can be a hidden, driven mechanism that comes out of you when needed. I believe this is an unexplainable thing that just happens in us.

# Chapter 15

Are you a caring person?

Either you are or you aren't. If you truly care about what goes on in your life you will do the right thing. To be caring you must have good qualities about yourself. I say being responsible is probably the most important one. This give you a standard to live by and the standard is your own because it up to you. How you live is determined by what you want out of life, from life. Don't look at other people, how they live look at what you are supposedly doing in your life to see both where you are coming from as well as going to I caring comes from when you were a child and that what your mother or father did for you will show as you grow to be older. Then you will see why you're doing certain things over other things you would not be doing as you grew up to be an adult. To accomplish anything in your life you would have to be caring. Caring goes long way-it tells others who you really are by what you do in your life and no one has the right to tell you one iota. I guess you can say that caring is part of the family values that are instilled in you from birth. On the other hand you can say you are he or she.?

# Chapter 16

Do you no right from wrong?

You believe in the right way of doing
things and you want them to be the correct way.
It is about being righteous and doing what it
takes to staying positive. We all make mistakes
in life but don't stay there. You learn by your
mistakes and you move on. People like dwelling
on the past tense but you have to let it go, go
forward. Think the future and look ahead to
the things you like to do, then go from there.
Keep good company and be grateful for your
friendships that are few along side life's journey.
Enjoy your life and be prosperous. It'll come
before you know it. Always remember there's
a wrong in doing things so remind yourself that

they can be corrected. Usually mistakes are made because  something happened in your life that you have no control over. Adapt and cope and you are all the better. Hopefully within time things will start to change for you. Believe that the things you do are for the better in your life, that someday it would be well worth the time and pressures because you were to foresee, life's endeavors.

# Chapter 17

Never place limits.

Don't ever give into setting limits on one. Think before you act, and then go seeking what you need to do. Try to discover new things that have been on your mind previously then see what you can come up with. Have a broad range and capacity in your thinking and see beyond the boundaries the horizon. As far as seeing yourself climbing the stairs by all means. Show others that making progress is rewarded in success. Limits is a negative word because you have most likely defeated yourself before you ever had a chance or started to getting things done that were necessary. As long as there are challenges for you in your life, there will never be an end to limits; they cannot be all fulfilled. No matter how much you try they can go on until doom day. How's that for an answer you've been looking for? Don't ever allow yourself to be mistakenly told there are limitations in your life; There aren't limitations. Man puts limitations on himself when they feel he has accomplished enough. Stay away from negative people. Their job is to bring you down, to keep you at their level. There is no other way they can think rational, for their thinking is off base. There's a never ending to limits so don't even go there. Believe what I just said and you'll be on your way to success.

# Chapter 18

There will be peer pressure.

It's coming and believe me, everyone that
you think is your friend is not your friend. I know
something about that; I've had some encounters
in my life. You will have some encounters in your
life because jealousy is coming, because this is
the way it is. No matter what people say about
you, don't let this get you down or worry about
what they say. Stay focused in what you are
doing, for the better. Do not lose concentration
or hope. Some peer pressure is good because
it reminds you who you are and you get to see
how other people really perceive what going on
around them. Peer pressure-everybody wants to
know what you are doing. Don't tell them whats

up, leave them in the dark. What they want to do is take your ideas, information and what ever else they get their hands on. Peer pressure wants you to get everything done perfect. There is no way you can or ever be, so don't even think about. Nothing is further from the truth

# Chapter 19

Be a good decision maker.

We all must have good judgment and no matter what, stand by your decision; After all, to come is where you're going to be asked, questioned by someone who didn't like your decision, why? Tell them because you had to make a quick decision  that had to be made and had to make this decision promptly, correctly, to the best of your ability. It starts with leadership; those other qualities that you have will go long way, toward your success. When it comes to making good decisions let face the facts: either you do, or you don't. The results are usually decisions that are made, meant to be. Furthermore, go with your gut feeling. Decisions are usually made by impulse; your instincts are the ones you must totally rely on. No matter what happens by the way, you're not going to satisfied everyone so why try any way?

# Chapter 20

Taking some risks.

You better do this with confidence and no turning back; go forward looking to attack the opening that is instilled in you and you bring it out of you to show others what you are made of. After all, get your share. Risk is good because it gives you a better chance to have the opportunity come before you now, then can you pursue. Sometimes when you're willing to take a risk, favor comes, and you find yourself in a comfortable situation after all.

# Chapter 21

Setting short-term goals.

Short-term goals are usually those within three to five years, because this allows you to learn all the company procedures, regulations and scheduling.

At the same time you're learning on a day-to-day basis, doing what is required. Short-term goals are good because you know that within the time frame a decision or decisions have to be made.

I believe a one to five year plan makes you more productive and accountable to produce the work you are accustomed to be doing in first place.

Setting long-term goals.

Long-term goals are good because you have time to endure and you know where you're going. Then the future allows the forecast to take place and you can settle for longevity. Now a days most jobs are safe for probably one to five years. After that I believe the economy and other economic factors take over. Long-term goals I don't think you can look ahead now a days, foreseeing what's coming. When it does the change, the process takes place right in front of you. The change came about with us, or without.

My question to you?

To succeed in life can happen. Your thinking is the key. There are no short cuts for success. Be willing to take a few risks along the way. Your journey is far but closer than you think. Let destiny have a say but remain focused to accomplish those desires you have set out to do for your life. My 21 pointers can only put you in the mood to be successful. Now it's up to you to execute the plan.

# Conclusion

The book gives detailed, precise techniques to show you how motivating is the desired factor for you to accomplish anything. Everything that is within reason can give the experience in life for everyday living. Choices and decisions must be done with confidence, with skillful determination. I say refuse the doubting if any comes your way. Offset the doubting with positive thinking by learning the positive steps I've given you to use: In return this should enable you to grow to higher heights than ever imaginable. Be always focused on a continuous track, knowing that success will come to you and others one day, because they never lost hope.

# About The Author

Melvin Lightford, B.S. Marketing has attended the University of Massachusetts-North Dartmouth, MA. President of Melvin Lightford Ministries, Inc. from 1998 to present. Retail management and Sales Representative from 1977-1980. Counselor for Department of Youth Services, Halifax, 1984. Brockton Police Dept. Brockton, MA, 1986 resigned in May 2005.